The Dark Edge of Europe

DESMOND O'GRADY

The Dark Edge of
Europe

*

POEMS

MACGIBBON & KEE

FIRST PUBLISHED 1967 BY MACGIBBON & KEE LTD
COPYRIGHT © DESMOND O'GRADY 1967
PRINTED IN GREAT BRITAIN BY
C. TINLING & CO. LTD
LIVERPOOL, LONDON AND PRESCOT

For
FLORENCE TAMBURRO

ACKNOWLEDGEMENTS

Some of these poems have appeared in *The Transatlantic Review*, *The Kilkenny Magazine*, *The Atlantic Monthly*, *Europa Letteraria*, *Burning Water*, *Studies*, *Poetry Ireland*, *The Holy Door*, *Botteghe Oscure*, *Arena*, *The University Review*, *The Irish Times*, *Threshold*, *New Poets of Ireland* (Alan Swallow, Denver, 1963), *The Castle Poets*, 1966.

Professor Kelleher and the Charles River appeared in a limited edition from The Carthage Press, Cambridge, Mass. 1964.

The selection and order of the poems is thematic, but a biographical order is also intended.

Acknowledgements are gratefully made to Acuff-Rose: The Chappell Group, for the lines from *Bye Bye Love* in the poem entitled "The Scattering".

CONTENTS

CONTENTS

THE DARK EDGE OF EUROPE

THE WORLD'S LOVEMONGER

In that hooked finger of bay,
With time displaced
Awhile from under a strong forehead
Of rock, we faced
Out on the hospitable sea
Simple as sand and childishly awkward.

Our savage blood in a rush,
The hot brass
Of the sun hammered us half demented
Till love was the grass
Coarsely welting our flesh
And the trudge back when the evening splintered.

While the whisper of love urging
Its crisis was all
The talk between us that year, and the awe
Of our bodies; while
Hardship was a childlike thing,
Not adult hate with a fixed jaw,

Some far-off place, unasked,
Some kind of killer—
Law was pushing a total stranger
Doggedly nearer
Till you in the end paid the cost
For a deal predesigned by the world's lovemonger.

WAS I SUPPOSED TO KNOW?

When,
In a blue-sharp, fallow sky,
With wind in hair
And grey of rock, angled by ages, sharpening the eye,
I
Stamped down that cut stone stair
Towards sand and sea
And clawed, nails scratching, down from deaf-mute cliffs to where
Were track and trees below—
Was I supposed to know?

When,
With senses quick as compass
And tightened skin,
In breaking clearing, fell on Church and Churchyard moss
I,
Helpless, toeheeled in
To Christ and Cross
And, staring staring silence, felt small as a pin,
Felt schoolboy years ago—
Was I supposed to know?

Was I supposed to know
That
Each fisted flex of heart
And wide of eye,
Each pitch of thought in bone-sprung skull; each stutter start
Of unravelled blood in my
Knit flesh and bone;
And every studied part I cast me as a boy;
That all my rebel scorn
And mock at prayer,
My every bedded bitch and spilled out kids unborn,
Were
All marked mine with care—
By some high Law

Or some high guiding Plan—to lead me back to where,
Again,
With coffin smell of pew
And criss of Cross,
Unwinking eyes of saints and hushed confession queue—
For one loud nervous boot
Of frightened heart,
I felt the Churcheyed, fidget fear of schooltied youth?

AN OLD MAN WITH AN OLD WOUND

He has kept it to himself for so long now:
Like some old pain as it were which, over the years
Has taken quiet advantage of arrears
In protest on his part and is familiar
Now as clocks; that still it has somehow,
Though marking time, become no more tired out
Than when at first it festered and broke out
Like sores, and turned for the safest healer
To a clean and bandaged silence of the heart.

HIS BATH

What is one to do when finally left to one's own resources—
Away from the system, the calls, the appointments—
With time, like one's shadow, all set at one's feet to carbon one's movements,
And no help allowed from exterior forces?

He slept through the long rest of the morning and rose for lunch.
Outside, in the first fold of the afternoon,
The day downed by the dare of the sun and the doped town
Thumped dull by the heat's punch.

Inside, the necessary meal consumed, the spotless utensils
Methodically back in their usual places,
The hour, suspended, no longer demanding on airs and graces,
Hung heavy at ease in the slack of its tensiles.

His last cigarette, before he undresses, at poise through his fingers,
The newspapers folded away from his reading,
The underwear waiting, the water, running into the bath like a bleeding,
Carrying out its inevitable filling—he lingers

Enough to see, for the catch of a moment, the man in the mirror
Is no one he knows, but an absolute stranger;
Enough to consider we're washed on arrival into the world
And washed on the day of our final departure.

AFTERNOON

Afternoon, and the houses are quiet as dust at the foot of a wall.
The tea and the coffee things cleared away from the talk and the thinking,
The magazines flicked through, the telephone tempting, the sand
in the hourglass sinking,
The waiting—knowing nothing will happen at all.

Afternoon, and just for the want of something more daring to do
Lunch is being seriously digested in the serious bowels of the town.
The buses are empty, the taxis unwanted and lorries are caught in a brown
Study of idleness. Business is slow.

In the parks and the playgrounds, shifty-eyed watchers in colourless clothes
Are hanging around like agents of death, while professional loungers,
In soft hats and silence, disinterestedly wait for the next observation;
and scroungers
And tricksters are nervously watching what goes.

Down by the shipless, motionless docks; abandoned by all
Except for a stray indefinable blur of what must be a man
And the inevitable rake of a pigeon scratching for corn; the cranes
Are struck dead—unable even to fall.

The voice on the radio—remote, unmelodic—gives news of events
And things that are happening—urban expansion, rural improvements,
Revolutions and riots, social reforms and new intellectual movements—
In lands with more future than this one presents.

In the lanes and the archways the children are few, the lovers fewer still
And those who are left have plans and intentions of joining the rest
On emigrant tickets. In the streets there is no one but old men and widows,
cursed
With sorry separation and a broken will.

Crack, and the shouts of men go up as a rat breaks cover
To die by the stones and the longhandled sticks of exasperation,
Back of the wagons in the stopped yards of the black, uneventful station—
And just for a moment the waiting is over.

TRIO

CONDITION

The most of us live at second hand,
And when, with hoots and shoves and raucous laughter,
You're driven out like some low scavenger,
There is at least, for all the panic after,
The final gesture of surrender—
A mad, frightened rush from the land.

At the end, the ineluctable sea,
Big as the waiting fist of the vital question;
And meekly, reduced to less than a whimper,
Aware there's no other possible interpretation,
You choose from the two jaws of the pincer:
Death imposed or death that's free.
    O our mothers do not love us anymore!

TWO POSITIONS

I : Lying in a Ploughed Field :

Something will never leave well enough alone.

Under the whistle clean sky—
The broad of my back
Worked into a drill in awkward mime
Of the country; Nature's cruelty
Forgiven; the smack
Of the beast in my loins—I lie till it's time
To trudge, resentfully, back into the town.

II : Suicide Lying in Death :

Pride has a set and satisfied look
In the impassive privacy locked in the posture of death.

Under more common conditions
The men would be there with their women,
Solemn as silence;
Dull with a peasant respect in the presence
Of the thing come without grudge or grievance.

Here no inhibitions
Distort this decision with even
Pathetic licence—
Dropped, like a stone, in the lone presence
Of the thing done without grudge or grievance.

SOLUTION

These small men, belted and buttoned up astern,
Bend to their sailing business deliberately as priests
And nose the long boat out through the local mists
With the tide grey and running on the slow turn.

The cliff line of the island lies like a small finger
Low along the far end of the muffled evening.
The mind no longer dribbles away and the soul's breathing
Has slowed and settled to a private, healthy measure.

At my turned back the madness of the town.
In my face a remote sanity of my own.

THE ISLAND

Like the eye of the liberating sea is my butt of an island.
In my house, cut from invulnerable stone
High on a knuckle of cliff,
With books for a woman, I live
Well rid of the baiting bitch of the land
And the sick spit of the soured town.

But when, like tonight in the storm, what's weakling fails
And hammers its grievance home in my head,
There's poor ease in rock,
Or sea, or printed book
From the gnaw in my mind and the single bed
That I'm left with since they stopped you dead in the run of your days.

And I pray in the heedless ear of the brooding night
For you back again; for your wild embrace
In the heel of the whitethorn hedge;
For the urge of your love on the edge
Of holy distraction; for the scourged pace
Of your demented talk of devotion blurring my sight;

For you back again no matter what's wrong or what right,
No matter that the old situation remains—
Stolen appointments on dark country
Gunbarrel roads, remarks
From old-watchers who live at their window panes
And the tongues of the craw-thumpers licking the scabs of their spite.

For I have grown tired of cultivating the soul,
Controlling the flesh, perfecting the mind;
Of working at words through the night
Till the eye's and the mind's sight
Give up—it's all no good, no good at all
When there's no woman to break and to bind.

THE LETTER

It arrived, as most letters do in a way,
Unannounced,
In the last post of the closing day.
The style of the hand,
Not childish, not grand,
Was still much the same—clutched up, unpronounced.
The postman who brought it, the regular man
On the street;
Glasses, moustache, a head like a can
And a limp; said all
The usual tall
Things of the weather, the taxes, his feet.

It began, in the slow and weighing hand,
Ruminations
Of times left behind long ago in a land
Of young understanding—
Times of unbending
Ideals and solemnly sworn dedications:
The strolls in the evening discussing the future,
The promises,
The essays, the books, the group-forming venture;
Society sittings,
Intellectual meetings,
The bold refutation of compromises.

But what with the time and the implications—
The prospects,
The living of lives, the communications
Gone rusty, unused,
The favours abused,
The old wild opinions reformed; suspicion,
Separation,
The intrusion of wives and personal ambition—
It had to be expected:
Too long neglected,
The course of events had destroyed the relation.

ENCOUNTER

Left
With the times I have known dragged after me like rags and rubbish in a
  perished sack,
With no single sign or telling how craftily the day that's tomorrow will turn,
With little gut to reason the ills or the justice that causes the crack
Between future and past by breaking wills and bending backs, I burn
With fear of the fin of the unquiet scythe
Relentlessly sweeping away at my side.

Once
Youth and love were a high stone wall and the tender protection of timber;
The house, the reverend quiet of the hall, the binding strength of the gables,
The sure sweep of the cropped lawn; every begotten member
Of family—solidly present as stone—gathered to eat at the table
And the feared fin of the idle scythe
Lying cold but quiet in the grass outside.

Now
By these mountains a moment, by this sane river the mind settles for spoils
On a child's pocket—a brass tosser, a bent nail, a badge,
A stub pencil, a polished nutmeg said to charm off boils—
Before sack and self can bundle up, legs steady and body lunge
On past the blearily finishing scythe
Intent on rebuilding what has been destroyed.

EPIPHANY

The face that stopped my eye
And stopped my day
Was not her face, and I
Saw in the way

Her bone was planed and set
No slightest match
Of vague resemblance, yet
For one quick catch

Of gasping time and place
Was vivified
What had long since lost face
But had not died.

Was vivified and shone,
Not like of face,
But what was antiphon—
Her air, her grace,

Her radiance and tone—
What fits no phrase—
What I had loved alone
In those young days.

THE POET IN OLD AGE FISHING
AT EVENING

FOR EZRA POUND

Comes a time
When even the old and familiar ideas
Float out of reach of the mind's hooks,
And the soul's prime
Has slipped like a fish through the once high weirs
Of an ailing confidence. O where are the books
On this kind of death?

Upright as love
Out on the tip of a tail of rock,
The sea ravelling off from the eye,
The line like the nerve
Straining the evening back from the clock,
He merges awhile into the lie
Of his own silhouette.

OVERHEARD MUMBLING TO HIMSELF
IN THE NIGHT

I

I would like to turn to you now in all sincerity—
Regardless of what sexless critic's frozen eye
May cast aspersion on what small conspiracy
May privately exist between us, or apply

To whatsoever calculated view of small
Coincidences: the school, the friends, a creed, upbringing;
I may, for some odd reason (you and me and all
We both together stand for) once have taken, meaning

You to stand for what you are and so much more—
But in that very turning, hope to find you gone
Beyond the unnecessary explanations we both deplore,
With all the gear of ceremony I have made you stand upon.

II

I'd like indeed to speak out now before this thing is done
And, if I can manage to, in slow simplicity.
Then I could feel we had it straightened out and, from
One point of view, with due account for modesty,

Feel sure you understand what you are now and how
(Because the way things were that curious year) I found
You first—raw as a rasher, crude as a stubborn sow,
With nothing more to recommend you than the ground

You stood upon. Then, perhaps, we both might feel
More quietly at our ease among the tins and cans,
The broken bricks and beaten walls that made us real—
If my crooked head would only say what my honest heart intends.

THE DARK EDGE OF EUROPE

I

A twist of cloth on the flat stones
Close by her heel in the rocky ford,
The peasant woman, bowed, unaware
Of the age on her back, the ache in her bones,
Washes away by the bend in the road
At the heel of the hill, a rag in her hair.

Farther behind in a yard full of haycocks
Her man and his son untackle the cart,
Stable the oxen, hang up the harness,
Their day done. One knocks
The crusted clay from the belly part
Of a shovel. The other stands in silence.

The valley suspends its diurnal labour.
Lake and island hang in the sky.
The sun, blocked by the broken wall
Of a castle, sinks with a stone's langour
Into the evening. The caught eye
Swivels to a hawk's impending fall.

By the butt of an ancient tree a boy,
My guide, squats sucking a stalk;
His head, his noble historical head,
Cocked like an animal's, his mind's eye
Fixed upon nothing. Out on the dark
Edge of Europe my love is dead.

II

Four years have seen some changes:
An average amount of general progress,
One laboured success completed,
A share of love, and that from strangers

[24]

An effort made to fit a place
In the system. Otherwise little of merit.

Four countries and four loves
Is what I look back on and no one of them
Quite understood or really concluded . . .

III

Nineteen hundred and fifty-six
Was the crucial year, with plenty of head
Pride in the heart and an open city . . .
Little more than child, the complex
That made her woman fired the mad
Longing for love in the university

Of my unschooled heart and I, being young,
Thought this the very stuff of passion
That makes endure what poem, or paint,
Bronze or hammered stone or long
Talk in the night can never fashion
Right or end the heart's complaint.

Was I to know that all her courage,
Before the year was fully out,
That all her musical accomplishment,
Her grace, civility, her carriage,
Were hers so that some drunken lout
Could knock her dead by accident?

IV

Other times and other places.
In a corner stands the only chair,
Its broken back spliced with wire.
The four walls reveal traces
Of dampness. The double bed by day
Serves as a table and second chair.

[25]

Crouched by the stove, busy with pans,
My lady, my blackhaired, sloe-eyed lady,
Prepares the evening meal; her hands,
Her flawless, innocent hands, stately
As alabaster. There is a wild
Flush in her face and she is with child.

O where do you lie this night, alone
With the doom of your love, your child and your sorrow
Alone with your ragbag of personal history,
Sick from the longing that gnaws at the bone
And the faces and habits of strangers, somehow
Surviving till daylight disperses the memory?

V

Then there's that Tuscan woman who
All her life has lived and loved
For the straight truth's sake and shared
Her house, her goods, her heart, her few
Halfpence with those who have since proved
Their worth, and asked no gratitude.

Maremma made her, Rome became her
And I have heard men tell who saw
Her cross a square a mere schoolgirl
That none could match her yellow hair or
Held-high head or grace in all
The city, she looked so rare and noble.

And I have seen her sit all night
By a dying man's hospital bed;
A man who could no longer speak
He lay so close to death; who with
His fist held hers and struck his forehead
Hard, he wanted so to speak.

A man she cared for twenty years,
To whom for twenty years gave all:

Faith, hope, love like a sister,
All the beauty that was hers,
Till death put final end to the whole
Lot and left her old if wiser.

O I have watched her in her house
With painters and with poet men—
The arrogant young, the old and famous—
In talk on every hand, cross
The room like a painted Florentine
Lady—watched her and grown jealous.

VI

Last of all there is you my child;
Last in line but first of all
With your long gold hair and Irish head,
Your high stubborn look, that wild
Way of yours, the magnificent pale wall
Of your forehead—proud as a pup of your blood.

I remember you with your three legged stool,
Your bits of coloured china ware,
Your broken doll and handful of polished
Stones, playing at house and school,
Talking to yourself like an adult. O where
Have all those simple playthings vanished

Now you have grown to writing desk
And copybook and pen, and wear
A white straw hat and blue kimono?
And for myself I only ask
Your love—now, and at the hour
Of my end . . .

VII

Up the crepuscular valley the night
Creeps like a great thieving animal.

The four women and one man
Working late off to my right
Have gone. There's no one left at all.
Somewhere a dog barks at the moon.

The boy, my guide, at the butt of his tree,
On the dark side of the castle wall,
Squats in his own shadow, his head
Bent, his eyes fixed upon me.
Somewhere out in the dark pall
Over Europe I leave my loves for dead.

THE SCATTERING

THE SCATTERING

FOR OLGA JWAIDEH

It would have been, had the toss of the thing fallen differently,
the side of the coin reversed, a simpler scene:
you proud in that magnificently peasant way, rehearsed
                          in the country's lean

give and take with talk, crossing the square
at evening under the eyes of the young rakes
of lads with their backs to the walls, their day in the fields
                          done. From flakes

of one of them's talk, caught by your selfconscious ears,
you'd mark him apart as a stranger come for work
to the district. In a place like this—with form the silence of elders
                          sucking a stalk

or a pipe at the corner, and the animal eyes of the young
single men pawing your thighs—so slight an encounter
would hold enough of the long rope of promise to tie
                          the knot in love's halter.

I

The universities scatter after exams.
Packed trains depart
for the passive provinces
A. M. D. G.
                Surrender the child for seven years
                do what you wish with him after
menticide in one generation
slings a glugger the next
                ad majorem Dei gloriam

The best in a generation salts its own statement
not dead men's slogans
nor their rags of slogans;

not the right cause fought
against the wrong people, not
                    an old bitch gone in the teeth
                        a botched civilization
and not the sanctification of false martyrs.
                    Qui tacent clamant

Terror triumphant
proclaims the *Resistance.*
A loser, the penalty's
for *offences against the State*—
not the state of things.
No questions. No explanations. No apology.
                    Qui tacent clamant

The freedom, the force
of a nation's sensibility
securely spancelled
by a sold constitution and six precepts.

Accept
and enjoy their hard-labour wage,
their priestly protection
ad majorem Dei gloriam . . .
                    Else take indelible nights
                    on emigrant ships
                    and the particular death
                    that involves
                        your tired, your poor
                    your huddled masses yearning to breathe free

At the corner of Ship Street and Golden Lane,
on the top floor over MacHughe's Public House,
the straw brass bed's left deserted—
The wardrobe door claps in the void,
table and shelves cleared of books and belongings,
the firegrate stuffed with stale fish-and-chips
and a dry whiskey bottle.
Finger-rubber into the windowpane dust:
Reilly Rotted Here

The day when heaven stoops his fire
we all hoist sail and stand
steerage and bags on the night ferry.

II

Monday morning opens the city
and money continues to breed
        the money-minded.
On the subway, the white-collared clerical officer
sits on his wallet of national health and insurance cards
        his briefcase, his private perversions—
                safe in the folds of his newspaper.
Beside him, the lovelorn lady
stenographer looks too far gone now for marriage.

With us there was nothing at cross purpose—
nothing of argument standing between us,
                in our basement bedsitter
                heart of a ghetto—
                the suitcases served us to work on.
That was in August approaching my birthday
and we daily went scrounging for work in the morning:
                in your eyes
        that look of minority groups
                and of emigrants
missing their customs, their climate, their rights.
        No Coloured
        No Dogs
        No Jews
        No Children
        No Irish
And at evening we'd meet on a bench in the Park,
        together go back to the room.
You've never had it so good, they said

                In August country now
                        lineal light
                        tips

[33]

gold in your hair slow
words on your bright
lips

hover on silver air
like birds
held

living to the hand where
soon your word is
child.

Fattened from war and the success of war
what's the complaint?
O
country to end all countries
O
system to end all systems
O
number in a file all one's own
O
number to end all numbers
in all files
always
O

The brown river god toils our filth to the sea.
The singer cries into the star falling night:
Bye bye love
Bye bye happiness
Hello nothingness
I think I'm agoing to die.
Where beats the compassionate heart of bureaucracy,
where throb those society membership cards,
    those multiple insurance policies;
who are the clerical officers,
    government administrators,
    military advisors
    paid to console,

                    to assure
that the fighting, the guns, the dying, the dead
                    and the left-overs
                    fit what's wanted?

        The only complaint, there is no complaint;
        that the great miracle-working, man machine
        works surely and mortally;
        that we've never had it so . . .

                        III

        Hotel du Midi quarante—sept rue Mouffetard
        with a view. Another top floor, a fiver
        a month for room twenty-two
        asked Madame Desage, with loving for heating.
        The river froze solid that winter,
        down by the Mistral Bookshop
        and two local *clochards*, Place de la Contrescarpe,
        one night followed suit—
        carried off stiff as sticks in the morning.

        When you can make it no farther
        they hammer you down to obedience—
        rather than hammer the system they serve
        and you pay for. We explain It hangs over
        from war. Hammer
        you into the stony green snot of their jails—
        the shine like a leer on the polished gun-holsters.
        There's no escape from the eye that burns
        the night from a cell.
        Which is the law, whose the morality?
        Who are the wives, where the family tables?
        Who are the loves?
                        And are we the children?

My sun goes down red as a roasted apple;
goes down upon vineyards and cattle and hard seamen

                        [35]

sitting below on a knuckle of rock handling their tackle
                    for the night's run—

down upon island women in black with burning faces
leaning in silence on terraces watching their men
in the boats leaving their crevices one at a time till the place is
                    still as when,

on a Sunday evening, they all trail down to the square
and into the church for prayer, and the last tolling
has died on the holy air and there's nothing more to hear
                    but the sea's breathing,

and all their voices hymn to the falling
sea and the same moon rising on the Aran Islands;
goes down on them there sizing each other up below the sea walling,
                    their hands in their trousers—

and my sun goes down on me in my room facing west
out of Procida over the breasts of Ischia, goes down
on mother and daughter lost in some London slum like the ghost
                    of Ireland, and down

on those left at home in Limerick on the Shannon River,
down on Dublin at the corner of Golden Lane
and Ship Street, down on rue Mouffetard and down forever
                    on us all in Rome.

SEPARATIONS

IMAGELESS IN AUTUMN

Almost the winter and nothing to speak of done
except what has been undone
and that I suppose will have to be answered for one day.
Meanwhile, perhaps it was all for the general good.
What has been done was, in a way, what we had to do
containing its own inevitability the moment we did it;
and if there's a question of blame or merit
it is due to the time and not to the individuals concerned.
A change in the time results in a change in the sensibility
and a change in the sensibility in a change of kind
in the love current at any particular time.
All we can ever be sure of
is that love in its nature is constant. How it presents itself
is of no importance whatever.

What we feel now is essentially
the same as we felt in the past
or may ever feel in the future; and yet
for some inexplicable reason, what was reality yesterday
is not necessarily reality today. And only God,
or his equivalent, knows what is coming tomorrow.
Whatever we did whenever we did it
was done of necessity, there being no suitable alternative:
first publication, the magazine venture,
the attic-room meetings under the roof,
the nights of loving or drinking, separation,
the current political crisis, talk of emigration,
lonely affairs with other men's wives,
resentment over the distribution of money.

The need that put us apart is the need that brought us together.

SIGHTSEEING

In the centre, the ancient churchyard, a national
Monument, giving out on a view of the valley
Where thickening hay, with the breeze like smoke
On its surface, gleams in the light like the brushstroked
Coat of a fairhaired animal—the bevy
Of crosses inclined to be lackadaisical

Like the spearheads of guardsmen at ease.
Not far to the left on a once moated mound
The exploded remains of a castle in motion
But petrified now at the point of disintegration.
To the right and down lower ground,
Hidden by beeches, some minor remains

With Romanesque portals in good preservation.
Ahead, and over the tufted grass
And the flagstones, between the bundle of bone—
Like crosses, the tomb with an old boot thrown on its topstone—
A touch of mortality—the deep boss
Of the river curves with a darkening motion.

Then after inspecting the architecture,
The doors and the windows, the restoration;
After tracing our fingers over the outlines
Left on the panelled stone by weather and winds;
With a mumbled-on-leaving appreciation—
Mere repetition of previous conjecture

On the state of a fragment—we move to the railing
For the car and the thermos of afternoon tea,
The chocolate biscuit, the sliver of lemon.
With the ancient locality as still as a woman,
The river getting on with going to sea,
We sip, while the castle holds back from its falling.

PROFESSOR KELLEHER AND THE
CHARLES RIVER

The Charles river reaps here like a sickle. April
Light sweeps flat as ice on the inner curve
Of the living water. Overhead, far from the wave, a dove
White gull heads inland. The spring air, still
Lean from winter, thaws. Walking, John
Kelleher and I talk on the civic lawn.

West, to our left, past some trees, over the ivy walls,
The clock towers, pinnacles, the pillared university yard,
The Protestant past of Cambridge New England selfconsciously dead
In the thawing clay of the Old Burying Ground. Miles
East, over the godless Atlantic, our common brother,
Ploughing his myth-muddy fields, embodies our order.

But here, while the students row by eights and fours on the river—
As my father used to row on the Shannon when, still a child,
I'd cross Thomond Bridge every Sunday, my back to the walled
And turreted castle, listening to that uncle Mykie deliver
His version of history—I listen now to John Kelleher
Unravel the past a short generation later.

Down at the green bank's nerve ends, its roots half in the river,
A leafing tree gathers refuse. The secret force
Of the water worries away the live earth's under-surface.
But his words, for the moment, hold back time's being's destroyer,
While the falling wave on both thighs of the ocean
Erodes the coasts, at its dying conceptual motion.

Two men, one young, one old, stand stopped acrobats in the blue
Day, their bitch river to heel. Beyond,
Some scraper, tower or ancestral house's gable end.
Then, helplessly, as in some ancient dance, the two
Begin their ageless struggle, while the tree's shadow
With all its arms, crawls on the offal-strewn meadow.

[41]

Locked in their mute struggle there by the blood-loosed tide
The two abjure all innocence, tear down past order—
The one calm, dispassionate, clearsighted, the other
Wild with ecstasy, intoxicated, world mad.
Surely some new order is at hand;
Some new form emerging where they stand.

Dusk. The great dim tide of shadows from the past
Gathers for the end—the living and the dead.
All force is fruitful. All opposing powers combine.
Aristocratic privilege, divine sanction, anarchy at last
Yield the new order. The saffron sun sets.
All shadows procession in an acropolis of lights.

ARRIVAL THE CAPITAL

After the five hour flight the confusion
    of stepping out to shake hands with the past.
No one to meet since nobody knows.
                        Almost a foreigner,
without excitement, with no apology, I brush
over scuttled faces crowding the barrier.

Secure as a diplomat in the taxi's corner I glide
through the suburban morning
        watching for changes,
                      suspended in Limbo.

Just as one left it. Children carrying bundles
or leaning dirty over the river wall. Mothers
strealing. Fronded canals clotted. Young men,
idle, backs to street-corners, unemployment,
                  emigration.

The city now, at its centre.
The years between us like ectoplasm.

                  My train down the country
and home not leaving till evening,
I tally old haunts, methodically—
                like one walks stones
in a familiar, abandoned churchyard.

Scrawn rake pigeons. The same skin-dry men
in pre-war topcoats (kippers for lunch
in empty briefcases) gently speaking aloud
to themselves.
                Countrymen up for the day
From the provinces to sales or the football:
"The enormous tragedy of the dream
                in the peasants' bent shoulders".

Down by the freighterless docks and the Custom House
the old characters still sitting alone in the sunlight—
bearded, spectacled, old age and rags,
sacks of books. Reading. A part of salvation
in private exile.
                        Her dog by the lamp post on Wicklow Street,
that crone woman still playing her harp,
but now to herself. Her husband
and with him his harp, has departed.
                            Indifferent students
coming from lectures or sitting about
on the Green: a new generation
                        avoiding old problems.
At intervals, shiftyeyed scroungers in colourless clothes
        around public urinals
                        and girls' school exits.
Out at suburban seasides I know
whitecollar workers on holiday, trousers
up to their knees, paddle children
in rusty salt water.
                        Along the seafront wall
in faded deckchairs, basking nuns
drain little warmth from a watery sun.
                        And weaving
like some geological fault through it all
those in control and responsible—
                        leaving well enough alone.
In public bars professors and such, in late
middle age, on their own, stare over whiskey thinking
                                nothing
in particular, considering
                        everything in general.
                                Waiting.
                        Nothing of matter will happen.
    Is patience the fringe of knowing?
About them, unheeded, the old conversations.

in that prominent corner, the flies
of his trousers unproperly buttoned,
grey hair sticking from under his soft hat
like black sheep's wool, a national poet.
                              I remember
an old poem beginning:
                              "If I went away
I should never come back".
        Somewhere outside, in their building-scheme lives
old friends are respectably settled.

I finish my drink. I leave for my train.
I go home to my provincial town
                              having spoken to no one.

HOMECOMING

The familiar pull of the slow train
trundling after a sinking sun on shadowed fields.
White light splicing the broad span of the sky.
Evening deepens grass, the breeze,
like purple smoke, ruffles its surface.
Straight into herring-dark skies the great cathedral spire
is sheer Gothic; slender and singular,
grey as the slate at school when a child looking up—
a bottle of raspberry in one hand, a brown bag of biscuits in t'other—
Feathereye Mykie my uncle told me a man
shot down a hawk dead from the cross
with a telescope fixed to his rifle.

Pulling home now into the station. Cunneen waving
a goatskin of wine from the Spain he has never seen
like an acolyte swinging a thurible.
My father, behind him, as ever in clerical grey,
white hair shining, his hand raised,
preaching away to the Poet Ryan.
And after a drink at the White House—out home.

The house in bedlam. He's here says my father.
Sober? my mother. She's looking me over.
Bring out the bottle. Pull round the fire.
Talk of the journey, living abroad:
Paris and London, Rome and New York.
What is it like in an airplane? my sister.
Glad you could make it—my brother.
Everything here the same tuppence ha'penny—the neighbours;
just as you left it; the same old roast chestnut.
After the songs, the one for the road,
the last caller gone—up to my room.

As I used find it home for the Christmas from school.
The great brass bed. The box still under it full
of old prayerbooks, assorted mementos,
the untouched bundle of letters mottled with mould.

[46]

Now it's a house of doorways and walls
and no laughter. A place for two old people
who speak to each other but rarely. And that only
when children return. Old people mumbling
low in the night of change and of ageing
when they think you asleep and not listening—
and we wide awake in the dark,
as when we were children.

READING THE UNPUBLISHED MANUSCRIPTS OF LOUIS MACNEICE AT KINSALE HARBOUR

One surely tires eventually of the frequent references—the gossip,
praise, the blame, the intimate anecdote—to those
who, for one unpredictable reason or other (living
abroad, difference of age, chance, the friends one chose,
being detained too long at the most opportune moment) one
never, face to tactile face, has met; but who
had the way things fall fallen favourably, once met, for some
right physic force, would have been polar, kindred you—
though time, space, human nature, sometimes contract
to force the action done that makes abstraction fact.

Here in this mock of a room which might have been yours, might have been
the place of our eventual meeting, I find a berth temporarily
(so long too late) among your possessions.
                                        Alone, except for your face
in the framed photos, I sit, with your manuscripts spread over my knees,
reliving the unpublished truths of your autobiography.
On the shelves and table, desk, floor, your books
and papers, your bundles of letters—as if you were just moving in
or out, or had been already for years—
like a poem in the making you'll never now finish.
Through the windows I see down to the hook of Old Kinsale Harbour.
Mid-summer. Under the sun the sea as smooth as a dish.
Below on the quays the fishermen wind up the morning's business:
stacking the fishboxes, scraping the scales from their tackle and hands.
Behind this house the hills shovel down on the town's slate roofs
the mysterious green mounds of their history.
Flaming fir, clouted holly.
Not an Irish harbour at all, but some other—
the kind you might find along the Iberian coast, only greener.

Down to here, down to this clay of contact between us, Hugh O'Neill
                                         once marched
from way up your part of the country, the North, the winter of sixteen
hundred and one, to connect with the long needed Spaniards three months
under siege in the Harbour. Having played the English their own game
                                         and watched
all his life for his moment, he lost our right lot in one bungled night
and with it the thousands of years of our past and our future. He began
what divides the North they brought your ash back to, from the South I
                                         have left
for Rome—where O'Neill's buried exiled. And here, then, this moment, late
as the day is (what matter your physical absence) I grow towards your
                                         knowing,
towards the reassurance of life in mortality, the importance, the value
                                         of dying.

COUNTRY WEDDING

FOR THOMAS AND MOIRA

I

The morning rush to get ready in town; my brother
the groom repeats, while shaving, my duties
as best man: "It's simple as falling". "I know,
I have fallen before". He cuts and draws blood
with the razor, sticks on a piece of old newspaper,
soaks up the bleeding. Our father, dressed up, attends
to the car like a white collar worker his afternoon off;
mother in search of her one false tooth; our uncle,
a widower never had children, refuses to come
and no explanation; nobody else from our childhood
at all but that gay woman who once
with my mother, when both were mere girls, watched soldiers
burn our house to the ground—One Corn Market
Row, the old part of town. She never got married . . .
Then off to the bride's parish church, a farmer's daughter,
in the dead heart of the country . . .

Their church unpolished granite. Her neighbours and people
seated left of the aisle: her father
is dead, her only brother grey prematurely at twenty,
her mother (who now rarely moves from bed) with a fallen
expression that has naught to do with the wedding. We
take the right, the young bride and groom the centre.
Up in the loft a tenor hired from the town singing.
The harmonium's wheeze. The old parish priest
the bride's great-uncle and famous the country round
for the night he caught some pair in the school house
courting and marched them five miles the road
straight home before him) unable to find
the page in the prayerbook, the case of his glasses,
water or wine, scolds the altarboy. I pass
the golden ring and silver dollar my brother
brought back from America to sink in a land

[50]

that never gave anyone anything . . .
"Do you take this woman . . ."

Once man and wife they walk down the aisle
to the stonepocked face of the fields, down to the dying breath
on the air of empty towns, out to their country.
At the church doors an old and anonymous crone
stops them to press holy medals on each
for what they have done and wish them male children.
Her own have long ago left her.

II

Later, out in the beaten sun and the open, milling around
as at market, we toast the bride, her groom
and all lovers. Up at the head of the table myself,
best man, calling the speeches with a foreigner's accent;
and over us all, like the shadow of cloud on a hill,
the great black priest.
Mothers are winding their business at opposite ends of the table;
the older men drink the land and the life it gives:
"Long life and death in our native country".
And then, with the blood like wine in our veins,
we clear the space for music and dancing.
Love in the head, pagan at heart, the green-eyed girls
clasp hands for the circle, spin the starched white
hoops of their skirts, the red of their petticoats.
Out on the fringe of the frantic music in black suits
young men lackadaisically eye the girls whirl
wild from the drinking, the marriage, the pleasure of male attention.

III

The burnt heart of their heathen sun
shrinks back in the mouths of their famished fields.
The parched tongues of their rivers turn
varicose blue in their veins.

Over the face of their female sky
their dark perspiration of blood spreads
yellow like rain on the face of their mountains.
Out at the raised eyebrow line of the wave,
slanting towards home over the blood-stained socket
of my saviour sea, a lone black wing—
like the dorsal fin out of the back of the shark—
heads relentlessly straight for the land
alone in her alien beauty.

THE NAIL

That unconscious gesture just then—the tilted head rolling
Against the chair's back, hinted by pain or distraction,

The subsequent silence left in the sentence, brings to mind
Dead spring days shot with fugitive light when I'd bound

Driven, a boy, through the hollow house to the stable
Yard, cobbled and closed as a prison's, where the indelible

Mouths of the coach-houses gaped four square about me. Tiering
Over my head the mansion of childhood disguising

Its terror, its mystery, its hourly demand for a cover
Of face to meet or present to its every dark cellar,

Casement and hallway, corridor, bedroom. Over
And out through the barred wicket gate my mother

Alone in her rose garden, her long white dress and her parasol
Turned head smiling and fixed like a photo—stuck full

With her personal notions concerning the process of love.
Her reserved potential for maternal hate dug her grave.

In the stables' lofts the stored fruit religiously rots.
In the wall through my damp hand a huge nail rusts.

The potting-shed clay congeals on the gardener's spade.
In my clutching fist the driven nail's rust flakes like age.
There's a time in the wound of childhood when something clots.

NATURA MORTA

Built, you remarked, by some foreigner,
your long, low house,
ochre faced, had box windows.
A house not of our part
of Europe but another: Tuscany,
Umbria, that valley
where Hannibal marched at the Romans—
Lake Trasimeno . . .

                      Your husband's
mother, the doctor, fading
like sunlight in her flower garden,
hardly at all as I remembered her.
The presence the same still,
and the cheekbones . . .
A doctor, she knew, I suppose,
about dying—in that particular way
Zhivago knew at the end, on the tram.

No rain this long while.

I sat by the overgrown mill-race.
You moved to and fro,
side to side of my retina,
shin deep in the racing shallows,
yellow hair down your shoulders,
paddling your children.
The long green weed on the stones
mythological hair
under the spangled water.
At my back the shell of the abandoned mill.
Mute granite. In my eye's corner
the family swan. Down at a distance
the kingfisher plunging and plunging.
Summer. The Festival of August.

The habit of ownership, belonging.
For that spliced moment we both belonged
to ourselves—and to each other.
Whatever stands still
gathers refuse—like the stepping stones.

My father sleeps in a hospital ward,
and perhaps he is dying.
My brother goes daily to work—
to work out his life and his death
in the land's oblivion.
Is there some relief in departure,
distraction in movement, postponement in going—
even backwards?
Or is it all like a stunned
crying out in confusion:
"Simpson!
Was that figure you I last saw
inviolate
crossing the river
into your own winter's garden
forever?"

WHILE VISITING CLONFERT
CATHEDRAL

I

Sinking, the sun's clandestine rays tangent
the eye. Ahead, the river crossed,
the ineluctable, modal West a fist
of Atlantic knuckles. This land is ancient.
On either side, the meadows, grave
with late afternoon, support the heavy
weight of early summer. Alive
overhead, the calls of the scaldcrow carry.
Down at the bend in the road appear
twin iron gates, tombstones, a tower,
the eleventh century Western door
of the church and a girl herding the pair
of her children home from their schoolday's labour.
The country in lead-lined heat (chestnut,
oak and yew, fruit and flower)
swells on the feeding earth to the root—
while the knowing salmon, like smouldering bronze
in her shallows, will burn the probing finger
and the ripening rose in its garden no longer
can hold decay back from the first petal's fringe.

Arrived, we pause outside the open
gates of the walled-in churchyard. My aged
companion thumbs in his old, back-broken
guidebook . . .
        Even here, despite the rich tillage,
live summer, the pulse of our pasts and our futures,
I change on sensing your absence—know
it is winging in like some dark seabird's shadow
over the agelessly earth-eating waters
to settle again on my spirit's shoulder
and, glistening black as the man-eating raven,
squawk out its fatal arrival, clutch tighter
its carnivorous claws, feed on separation.

But I have come here for distraction—to forget
I lived with you years in another country,
took on your problems, responsibilities,
practised your way of life, and yet,
for those very reasons even, decided
to leave in the end, although there was nothing
at cross purpose between us . . .

Gerard

Ryan, my companion and guide, in his virgilian
voice reads from his guidebook aloud and we buckle
down to inspecting the tombstones and chapel:
". . . . Brendan the Navigator founded the original
sixth century church where the present cathedral
stands . . . " and we move from the dying glare,
through the open gates beyond which a frantic
scatter of butterflies battles the air
with a blind futility like the hopelessly manic.

I I

The day within the churchyard's separate somehow;
all sense of time, cubic space, tactility
(rank wilderness of grass, the sultry growth
of summer feeding on the dead, row
on crooked row of rain-wrecked stones and ivy
eaten crosses) extend beyond the face import
of their own inherent restrictions, compass the general
past of a race in the thousands of years of its history
and suckle the starved mind's tendrils kneading greedily
the ages' abundance for sustenance. Here death is optical
only: not the force that causes the change in temporary
matter, the gases' escape, liquefaction—the invisibly
living power of the body dead and buried
and rotten; nor the dying process of the mortally living.
This should then be consolation (the mind's distraction
from the daily bleeding to death after death from the ragged
wound that's the pumping sense of your absence in the turning
world outside) the vision of history's action
in the visibly present, reducing the flesh's importance
to zero, augmenting the intellect's insight . . .

                                                                    I turn
then here to my worldwise companion Ryan as once
to Professor Kelleher, and again, at a farther distance,
in childhood, to my uncle Mykie, and through them discern,
farther back, history's Brendans—my ancients', my ancestors' presence.

ENVOI

The securer mind sinks a fresh foundation for the hesitant
blind heart's dependence: the past is present, the present
past and the heart strives daily, like some winged merman,
to navigate the most relevant, personal course between them.

DEPARTURE

You left alone at the rail watching me walk
to the plane. The breeze catching the white of the dress
you wore the evening I returned so bronzed
after the summer and told you all my adventures.
The plane with an awkward grace on the ground
out of its element. Behind me the myths of your face
sinking like ships in our separation. Around us
our years, now seconds, together:
the night we helped the old poet die in the hospital
bed and with him a part of yourself we later
resurrected between us, gave life to, made love of;
the depths of our nights together in my old-fashioned
furnished apartment or out on the open
side of a hill in a rush under the eye
of the all seeing moon in the spring;
our daily appointments each afternoon for a drink
down in the corner at Albrecht's.
At times, after love or a difference, I spoke
of this day and this parting—not really believing.
You forgave me my weakness.

I cross the burning flats of the tarmac afraid
to look back. Your image the white of the sun in my eyes.
At the door of the aircraft I wave like a schoolboy.
I buckle the belt for a safety no longer desired.
Taxi for take-off. A moment of revving.
Expectation. Then the off the up the banking away
deeper into your life and my own
than I ever went into your body.
Away to an alien room in another country
surrounded by strangers to write this down
like a late entry in an old diary.

MEMORIES OF AN INFLUENTIAL UNCLE

'Ah, my dear children, why do you look at me like this?'
EURIPIDES: Medea

'and yet, and yet one word
Makes all those difficulties disappear.'
SOPHOCLES: Oedipus at Colonus

I

In a crow black suit you'd confuse for a beggar's, grey hair combed
flat and straight across his head,
he stands in the door of his condemned house, bronzed
fists in his coat pockets, spit grey eyes
no brighter, no bigger than nailheads. In his forehead
a small deep dent from the shaft of a backed-up cart when a child.
Away over the rooftops and pigeon-lofts, the spire of St. John's
Cathedral. Straight in front, his slum
inheritance—his mother's empire. Over his head
the three floors of the old house that bred
the lot of them, still furnished, its harm
done. Forty years of dust on the sheet covered forms.
Up in the rat looted attic black sea trunks, still standing half open,
packed with the wardrobe he wore on those Indian
cruises after his mother's death and her will.
Not a penny has seen daylight since. He moved to a small
house in the country and spoke to no one.
He married late and she died early. He remained alone:
his position with contemporaries always the blind side of form, playing rare
and wise in his silences—a kind of hostility.
He was tight with money, superstitious, secretive, cold
as a herring when driving a bargain, honest as salt.
He feared his God, but distrusted his clergy.
He returned unchanged from his cruises and never again went anywhere.

But for me as a child, in that long toyless night of the War, his presence
was brightly Homeric. While Hitler's Huns
converged on the Channel and Goering came nightly to hammer
down Coventry, I sat by the fire while he told me of other
times and their heroes: the mad Black and Tans
or Cuchulainn, O'Neill, Dan O'Connell, or Niall of the Nine Hostages,
the Children of Lir or the Wooing of Emer, the Salmon of Knowledge
or the Story of Deirdre, the Coming of Patrick,
the Three Sons of Uisneach, the Return of Ossian or Death
of Cuchulainn, the Danes and the Normans, Hogan the Poet
of Thomond or the ballad The Blacksmith of Limerick,
the Civil War that divided the family, my grandfather's plunge
to ruin and death from his drinking, my grandmother's curse on his sons'
children. He distrusted success and any characteristic
trait of a questionable ancestor. His greatest hate
was proud independence in youth, or any sign that might
lead to it—frequently warning: individualistic
action from pride could only end badly—and cited relations.

In the natural, if unbalanced, struggle between generations we form
an unworded, life-long alliances of forces:
the older delivering oracles, the younger interpreting—
simply at first, but with more complicated, harrowing
subtlety later till the final phase is
compulsive dedication to living these oracles through to their dénouement.
So that, time after time, down that long black night of our northern winter,
he would lead me helpless to that dark ledge
of the heart's land's end (where the soul's black sea, like an epileptic,
works out its ceaseless agony far below, and the frantic
seabirds scream and wheel at their scourge)
and he'd show me a vision of the lost soul's torment in ultimate failure.

But now that the adult eye has its own perspective and human
fear and the heart their own reservation,
I dimly see through the dark significance his presence
held then for the trusting child—oracular in the province
of his native caution, his mystery and notion
that the sins of our ancestors inevitably fall on the lives of our own.
We all sail sightlessly out to our own self-wreckage, and years
later, in far away cities, when the lean
north wind goes loping the streets like a grey famished animal
hunting for something to claw and devour, when maternal
need casts a shadow like crime on the town,
when fathers are dead at the hands of departed children and laws
that achieve their own order give us marriage and offspring, we live out the
                                                                          word
of our ancestors warning irrevocably, and consummate
our own private ruin—for the dead slay the living in turn.

And is there then no escaping? Is our final salvation
our love's condemnation to failure in spite
of the will to choice and to action, and the will to negate the absurd?
Whatever the consequence, to attempt the impossible, step off the ledge
of restrictive inheritance—this is not failure;
but failing to act for fear of the failure in consequence . . .
The heart's obligation to the soul's vision and sense
of the self—its satisfaction; our
degree of decision given chosen action; may alone be our judge.

VALE

Now, a far lost cry from the coast of my origins, my final rest is
at last by this ancient equestrian statue.
I blindly face west to what's now my uncle's kingdom.
My lone daughter's image surrounds me. Who needs a tomb
once terms are made with love's reasons? Who
is not his own instrument blindly seeking his known final peace, his Colonus?

[62]

INSTEAD OF A LETTER

FOR GERARD RYAN

'What thou lov'st well remains, the rest is dross;
What thou lov'st well shall not be reft from thee
What thou lov'st well is thy true heritage'
    EZRA POUND: The Pisan Cantos; Canto LXXXI

I have come to stay for a while
In this part of the country, famous
For its castles perched on impossible peaks,
For its masterful mountains and
Small churches with wooden rectangular steeples.
I had wanted to write but then
So much has happened since last we met:
Countries you have never seen, people you have never
And will never meet; so many decisions
To be faced and taken;
Good times to be had; new kinds of stress
And distress; new kinds of happiness
And you, I suppose, have since married.
I well remember the day you met—
The students were coming from lectures
And it was late in the spring.
I think we talked of my leaving.

It is weariness of the North
That drives us into the South
Where the wine-warm sea brings out in us
Sentiments not unlike love of one's country.

Here among mountains I long to be down by the sea.
In the mornings I write a little and read
Out on the back terrace, stopping at times
To look down, over the tops of the high pines,
Into the warm cleft of the valley. The clouds
Are always dramatic about the distant peaks.

E   [63]

Yesterday I walked down by the lake and watched
The fierce boys hunting for frogs with catapults
And an ardent patience;
Watched them chase the regal dragonflies
Round the fronded edge of the lake with sharp
Shouts of life. To remain young we only need do
What young people do. And later I walked
Home through the woods hoping that surely
Today there would be news.
But no. Only the newspaper.

Although it already is autumn
And the first snow has arrived
On the highest peaks in the distance,
The crocus is out in the cut meadows
And there is a strong scent of mown hay.
For you the crocus came and went in the spring.
Here, with the shadow of winter
Imminent now in the face of the mountains,
It is like a second or false spring.

Although there is plenty of sun
I know it is cold in the shade.
There are few birds to be heard
Now that they cut
The trees down daily. Soon I suppose
They will be gone forever
And only the whites of the houses
And bare rock will be left.

Rarely do I get letters
From old friends. And the newspapers
Do not tell one much.
You I suppose have children by now.

In the evenings I sometimes walk
Down through the woods for a drink before dinner
Passing the men returning home from the fields
Their women carrying loads on their heads,
Baskets strapped to their backs,
Scarfs round their necks, their children
Trailing behind in the dust of the road.
They salute me in turn in the name of God.
Their oxen wear bells that twinkle all over the evening.

And every day like a child I hope
To see you, or one of our old friends,
On the roads walking to meet me.

The first snow has appeared and I
Am tired of being alone;
Of speaking another language
Of being another person.
Although at times, at evening, after the sunset,
The mountains are coloured like those in the North.
But there never is any rain.

Soon the farmers' boys will come out
And crack their long whips to each other
From mountain to mountain,
The echo thrown back from the purple horizon
And up from the floor of the valley;
And then I must go indoors out of the chill
For dinner, and idle talk with the others.

On feastdays they hold a holiday
Down in the village, with music and wine
And dancing in costume;
The girls laughing and spinning
Up on the dancing platform heads
Thrown back in excitement; the young men
Stiffly prancing and proud from their drinking.
But I do not go down any longer.
The happy shadows of lovers
Under the trees in the night
Have become an embarrassment to me.

[65]

And I sit in the house,
After we've eaten, and write
All this to you finally.
In the morning the boy
Will take it down to the village with reverence
Like a small urn containing my ashes
And send it away to you.

LAND AND SEA

THE SEAMAN'S FLOWER
IN THE GARDEN

Out of the shellfish morning
Out of the doving foam
Your loving mouth, like the opening grave,
Lips in the fossiled breast the white
Bones of the heart's small bird.
> *The feel of your face in the folding eye*
> *Behind the seaman's flower in the garden.*
Down through the church-going morning,
Down through the wrongs in the dark
The shark of your love follows my grief
Like the fisherman's woman in black prays
For life against ocean and blood.
> *The beast at your breast golden and green*
> *Succours the heart in its hurricane cage.*
Out of the maid of the morning,
Out of the mater sea
The tongue of your love like the fish in the wave
Dives to its bed through my seawild head
And drowns in mythology.
> *The harp of your hand on the prowling sea*
> *Sifts the sand from the beloved skeleton.*
Down at the oyster's yearning,
Down at the morning's eye
The sun tips up like an angel's wing,
Strikes for love through the breaking dawn
And opens the mystery.
> *The heat of your hand on the day's rim*
> *Delivers us now through our holy rage.*

LAND

FOR CARESSE CROSBY

The new-born child, precious as platinum, fairer
than gold, nearer and dearer than his first field
is to the land-wedded farmer—grows like a flame in the warmer
parts of the chilled

hearth and cold stone of love's lost labour
until like the burning babe, turned ash for the old,
it opens to swallow whatever has twisted the blood in our
brains, that our coupled

days and muscled nights be blessed and protected
from all that the longing neglected have slept with and cursed
in their matrimonial death beds; grows and uncovers the hatred
and suffers the most.

O blond dove child! O living kiss begotten!
Whether made from the crest of the knocking wave or come wild
from the thigh of the loving locking or, far from the sight of the sun,
from under the field

deep at the heart of the darkest water and stone;
whether you are daughter or son—part of my part,
flesh of my blood and my bone—for you, for you alone
do I make this start

at circumscription. So come to me here this day
a longing loved way from the sea and the holy passion
of times that were, in their way, gilded with innocence, and stay
with me through my devotion.

Come to me here in this house of the millecento
crown of Roccasinibalda, navel of Italy
and the country Hannibal marched through going to Rome
two thousand years before me.

Come to me here on the borders of Umbria and Tuscany
in the night of this grave country alone with my spectre
of truth and a dog distantly barking; alone with my history,
my sexual gear

and my only company that ancient peace loving muse
La Bianca, blocked from abuse in her gloom, come to me
full of what passion you choose and pull out the handful of truths
of my autobiography . . .

Down in the valley under the star and the roof
beast and peasant move in their sleep. The coiling
serpent moves on the turf, the dark bull stamps with his hoof,
limp loins stir slowly . . .

Tonight the proud young husbandman lies straight
as a spade by an open gate, feathering blood
with the lovesick faith of an acolyte in the curdled cod eye of the great
feminine bird

till the child in his head, like a flying fish, sails out
through the ring in the tossing cot of the married dead,
out from the hulk of the heart to its doom in the downfalling doubt
of the wedding word.

O why can't the heart—as the tree spirals up in its bark,
the grass curls stalk in stalk, the river lies quiet
in the folds of the hills and the dark lies fast in the hold of the dark—
quieten that part

of the lone heart's night where one's lost vainglorious dead
loves rage at the senseless head that denies them the right
to what they love well, and quiet the need of the husband in bed
with himself for a bride?

O the law of the land is the same for the hunter and hunted,
and the beast that is best is what's wanted. Out where the hand
that rules is wholly against it and the hand that serves can't prevent it,
love is struck dead—

[71]

and the husbandman's shout in the wood dark world for life
is the homelessly crying for wife to the night, caught
and stopped with the loving knife in the kissing mouth by the grief
impaling the heart.

Hunter and hunted he runs through the world's mad wood
with his need on his shoulder like blood, to the wanting and wanted
until, like an ambusher should, she finishes him off for good
with her love and her hatred.

O husbandman, husbandman, lord of the nail and the hammer,
open your eyes to the grammar of lies a woman
will wrap round your marriage finger in the most aphrodital manner
to bed you, and then

in the digging disguise of the copulate dark, be the fake
butt of your fury and shake the wool on your thighs.
o bury your love for your own sake in the chances love cannot take
and button your eyes.

GIRL AND WIDOW ON A
SEA PARK BENCH

In this park by the sea, marvellous
As marble, under the fronded green of the palms,
The sun strafing
The stones with flat tracers of light, water like mercury
Tinnular out of the fountain;
You come to me out of the gold stained day like a word—
Come to my chambers
Of vacancy love has left in the haunted halls of the heart.
> *Our love is the metal in seagulls' eyes*
> *Plunging for plunder the faces of water.*
With the sun high over the mountain,
The idle light held in the air like a bird,
The day saunters
By, like a seaman waiting for tide and the evening's start;
And you, with the distance between us
Green as the secret seas of our separate calms,
Are youthfully laughing
Away, for the widow beside you, the black weeds of her misery.
> *My hope is the hour in your harbouring hands*
> *Or the sea as she harbours the hearths of her houses.*
At their ease, like the movement of palms
Over my head, the indolent children, frowsty
From school, fuddle
About in the sunlight over here by the seafronting statue;
While you, your unheard laugh
And your widow, sit alone in the day's shadow
Stretching across,
Like a black sail spread for drying, the ground between us.
> *Yours is the power of the ocean's slaughter*
> *In the foam unfolding away from the bows.*
Permit me then on behalf
Of all our dyings of yesterday, your widow's tomorrow,
My daily loss
In the sight of your absence, to reach to you over the murder
                              between us

[73]

Into our separate qualms
That I might throttle the threat of our grief with the thirsty
Tongue of the killable
And breathe the love of all the world back in the heart of you.
> *Our death is the point at the action's crisis*
> *When the shark's sharp tooth on striking, clings.*

MOUNTAINS

Let these rock ruined mountains reassure
The stony magnificence of our castle
Size love that borders like boulders
Our hearts' safe estate, reassure
The wrath hammered rage of our bodies'
Blood blessed demesne, go winter
Come summer; let the land's clay pronounce
For us surely as springshine the whispering
Pledges we cast on the wind
Up each valley's flues, year making
Merciless year, fear sunrise
Praise nightfall; pronounce like a crier
Love's winging wide outbreak, covey down
Doves from the eaves of our hearts'
Holding household, firm on its bedrock
And war for our one body's keep!

Draw succour, drain source from the eagle far
Season hurt holdings that hustle
Like lovers between the hills shoulders;
Praise the priest ordained peasant the more
Since the lone ploughing farmer priest honours
Our hearts' host sown deep down our mother
Earth's trumpeting womb, and pronounce
Consummation when the urgent sea's billowing
Blows live through the valley, joins kind
In the forked farmer's hearth at his making
And settles our saviour come sunrise;
But prepare when love's glance notes its hour
Death's darkling last wicks for our gloom
Warmed bodies cursed changing of parts
When we pass proudly out to last wedlock
And rest in a cypress of sleep!

SEA

In each blind gloom 'the gold will gather the light against it',
   Draw sight from the eye through the smouldering dark, remould
The beatified face for a time in the palm of its feminine heart and honour
   With vision the reverent presence who prays
   For release, or half a trance
   Of deliverence, through the sacred glance.
O valuable metal, O golden girl as the morning rising,
   Look down—regard the humility of your footman and grant
Your forgiveness, that he and his crime may come back to your own from the
                                            gloom, see you
   Fair as the moon again, serve your commandments.

I

Beyond my seafacing window and the *persiane*, the poker eye
Of the risen sun burns through pine to the iodine heart of the poppy
And the seminal clay where our bed was once in heat with a different year,
And the consummate sea through the holy day whispered love's prayer in our
                                                                    ear:
Forgive us our madness and give us this day the need and the will to try.
O under whose sun now on whose clay do you burn away from me
Selfish as silver, proud as a boy in the maw of the thralling sea.

II

Things will speak for themselves in the long run or so I helplessly hope
This jejune morning. The wine-soft sea, these marble inset mountains
These ochre houses and cobbled rivers will all silently grope
For stony speech that we—when the size of the word still detains
Our tongues from its utterance—might forgive and forgo the heartless hour
of love's ending
And burn in the solace of the sister sea and the mother massive mountains.
O take you then this country of my body love for healing.

III

Here again like specks on the knee of Italy at the day's good ending
With the same sun still pretending there's God and the copper pines
                                                    attending,
We walk by the self-same sea that swallowed him, his heart and his madness
Easy as marble and now is swallowing me and you—or what's left of us.
O why can't the thurible act that turns the sand into grain or gold
Return to honour the hour and alter our death in the heart of the world?
Pale lady, grant your grace and breathe your word into me.

IV

Day weakens and over the failing crepuscular wave the light
Makes way for a fecund brood of stars as the fisher boats fumble towards
                                                                                home.
Along the broken toothed wall the gold embroidered sea,
Sacred as a ceremonial vestment, is alone in the silent nave of the night—
O I have learned too late too late from the bark or worse from the bite
Of that mad bitch whose smothering love is the fit in the prayer in the poem:
To master *la morte* we daily must die of the madness and prides of
                                                                        despondency.

V

Down the cathedral sky the hooded monk of night still
Watches the holy world and broods over the face of wisdom;
The cameo moon, like the goddess behind your unkindness, continues to
honour
The eucharist hour and reflect me the sight of my oral soul in the sea;
And I pray to you out of my wrong and my right in the flame of what we have
done
To soften the fear the heart cannot hold and leaven our love from the marrow
That we might burn of earth in the bone and sink in the primitive sea.

VI

Like the golden boy dives through the eye of the pearling sea for the grain
That stings at the heart of the oyster, my nubile thought follows you down
The fjords that midnight has cleft in the watery evening, noble yet fearing
To find in the hulk of your sunken face the horror that love has an ending;
Follows you down to the stolen night when the moon and its star like a lover
Rose from the sea through your time-long hair, entered the hollow of heaven,
Reached past the hold of the darkling world and poured in its light till we

died.

VII

Out where night like wings is unfolding and the farmost star is falling
Down from the ocean dark through the first bronze wave to the fishes waking
Under the palms of their miracle; out where the flesh is woman and water,
Goddess and godless, mother and daughter, the merman sun is rising
Triton and golden out of love's ashes and the smouldering bed of the sea.
No fire can burn the feathered resurrection rising to find its own altar
Out where the twilight gong of the dawn delivers the boy from his thigh.

EPILOGUE

O let her again rise naked and spinning out of her chaos
   And finding nothing of substance to stand on, let her
Divide the fickle seas from the holy ghost of the sky and dance
       Alone over the lovely wave
       Until—like the lecherous dove
       From brooding on water clove
Through the serpentine air, the vine in its tooth—she can settle for us
   And for all on the breast of her mountain maiden and mother,
Whose blood is the fire in the feathered heart of the lover; who kills
                        at a glance
     The man at the foot of the bed and the grave.

YEAR'S ENDING

This heathen's own heather, our blood brown westering boglands,
  Rolls out from the weathered eye into the late day's
Declining. No bird wings the sea. The heard bell's St. John's.
  We've come prodigal ways.

Here strikes no cold careless arm, aimless in love,
  Of some passing clayshod, fieldwedded lout
Dazed by the land dream's own ruin; gives ground no flawed nerve
  That's the baffled man's plight

At the lost heart's displacement, nor stretches one desperate grope
  For love's reachless straws loose on the hour's tide.
Here cries out no crocked passion pedlar's shocked plea to support
  A heart with no bride.

But here, where our river realizes its sea and our landsend
  At last shingles into the sand and our town
Sinks its towers in the river's green rapids, we bind safe the wound
  That cut parting's incision

And heal the heart's long hidden hurt of this absence; we pronounce,
  Like apostles before consecration, love's prayer
When the sacred seed bursts like a saviour in season, and rejoice
  In the passion we share.

The one-legged seagulls still stand on the mute granite walling.
  Our brothers still brazen the blind land's oblivion.
The dark boats that bear the what's left of us leaving are sailing.
  Our year's song is done.

[85]

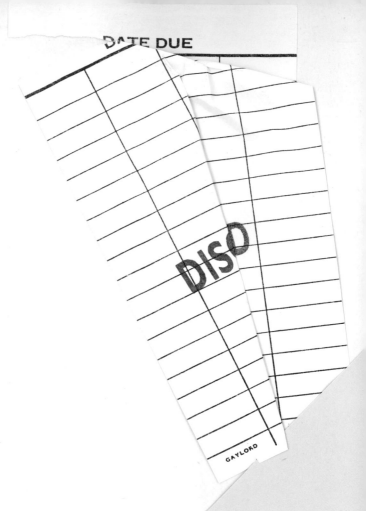